CW00864455

Interview Preparation

Deconstructing the Interview Process

Philip Charsley

Contents

Introduction

This book will hopefully provide you with a better understanding of the structure that the interview process is built upon and how you can use this knowledge to optimise your interview skills and improve your performance at a job interview. It is actually based on a process that most people are not cognisant of, yet use every day in a multitude of scenarios. It is based on how we develop relationships with people.

My hope is that if you bought this book on a Friday and read it over the weekend, you'd be fully prepared for an interview the following Monday.

About me and this approach

I have worked in Banking and Financial Services recruitment in London since 1999. During this time, we've had Economic Downturns, Dotcom Bubbles & Credit Crunches and the recruitment market, like everything else, has been extremely unpredictable throughout. Early on, it was clear that if I only got one job to work on for the week, I had to make absolutely certain that every candidate I put forward was going to be prepped to the best of my ability.

The approach I developed I refer to as Interview Coaching rather than basic preparation. Interviewing is not something people do every day and a generalised list of 'Do's and 'Don'ts to prepare with isn't enough to go on. That was the principal reason I decided to write this book: to eliminate guesswork and get people really thinking about how to give the best of themselves during an interview.

Years ago, it became clear to me that what every individual needs to target during an interview is the impression they leave on the hiring manager. The employer's perception of the individual is absolutely key to progressing through each stage of the interview process. So what do they look for? Is there a pattern that employers typically follow? Is there anything that employers have in common when interviewing people – no matter whether the job is for a Data Entry Clerk or a Managing Director? Happily, the answer is yes…there is a pattern that almost every employer in the world follows and almost all of them don't have a clue that they are following it. As I mentioned above: it is all about the way we develop relationships and you will see how you can use this to your advantage.

I sincerely hope that the information in this book supports you in landing the job you've always wanted. Investing a few hours to read this and most importantly think about yourself and how you are perceived, will improve your interview performance considerably.

Here are some valuable truths to consider:

- **Well prepared candidates have more confidence, creating a better first impression.**

- **Well prepared candidates provide better responses to interview questions.**

- **Well prepared candidates get better salary offers.**

Interview Preparation

Deconstructing the Interview Process

A Word on Relationship Building & Social Conditioning

Understanding the behavioural structure that underpins the way that people interact when they meet for the first time, is a fundamental element to being successful in an interview.

When preparing for interviews, I think it is essential that people pay close attention to the behavioural routine we always go through when we meet a person for the first time. From birth, we are programmed to interact with people by following the lead of our parents, peer group or mirroring the behaviour of people in our immediate environment. We learn to adjust our behaviour accordingly and over time, gain a full understanding of the social laws that apply within our environment, culture, society etc. It is these rules that guide us when developing a relationship with someone we don't know.

There are two schools of thought when it comes to forming relationships:

1. Something that we cannot influence; we are pre-conditioned as a result of our childhood experiences and basic instincts **or**
2. Relationships are formed through the social skills that we acquired and developed through education.

In the context of interviewing, I think both have equal merit. We use our pre-conditioned instincts as well as our acquired knowledge to interact with our colleagues and employers and manage the relationships we develop with them. In order to impress an employer at the first meeting, we use a complex system of verbal and non-verbal communication skills that we have individually developed that will hopefully leave a positive first-impression on them. It is equally important to consider the signals you receive from the employer during the conversation: Positive? Negative? What are they?

It follows that a great deal of importance should be placed on understanding the mechanics of how all of us develop relationships and how you can use this knowledge to interview far more successfully than you have previously.

Throughout this book, I will refer to the analogy that an interview is very similar to going on a blind date. After all, a blind date is meeting someone for the very first time just like an interview. It's uncomfortable, awkward and nerve-wracking but made a whole lot better when you've prepared properly and know what to say and more importantly, **what not to say**!

Deconstructing the Interview Process: The Clock

It might surprise you but almost all interviews follow a very similar pattern, no matter if you're going for a job at a Coffee Bar or an Investment Bank. It's obvious that the purpose of the interview process is to meet you, understand more about you and assess whether you are the type of person that can perform the job well. Depending on the level of the job, this can range from a quick chat and an offer to a full day of occupational assessments and numerous qualifying interviews. Dismantling or deconstructing the entire interview process will give you a much more accurate picture of how you are being assessed by the employer.

The Clock

Generally, most employers will dedicate one hour of their diary to conduct a professional interview. In that hour they should have more than enough time to decide whether to proceed to the next stage or not. But here is where we look at the sequence they are following in order to make their decision. Most people never consider this and it is the single most important tool you have to ensure you do well at interviews.

To describe the sequence in which interviews are typically conducted, I created a diagrammatical explanation that I call 'The Clock' that outlines the critical points that dictate how our 'social conditioning' works in order for us to develop relationships - whether it is in a job interview or meeting someone for the first time.

The Clock

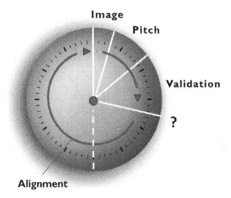

The sequence of steps is outlined as follows:

1. Image - How you present yourself
2. The Pitch - Why are you relevant?
3. Validation - Interviewer questioning
4. The 15-20 minute rule? - Are you right for this role?
5. Alignment - Sharing information & interests

Our 'social conditioning' means that no matter how long we spend with someone for the first time, we will almost always follow a pattern that helps us determine whether we like them or not. It is the same for determining whether the person we are interviewing has the right experience and qualifications we require for the job on offer. We're looking for people who share similar values and that is why deconstructing the interview process makes sense.

How it Works

If you consider that the employer has reviewed your CV /Résumé[1] and compared it against others received. Then you get a request for an interview, which must mean that he/she believes that you are a contender for the role they have to offer, right? Otherwise, why would they be inviting you in to their offices? So you should gain confidence from the fact that you've beaten most of the applicants, now you just need to beat the shortlist.

Now contrast this with a blind date arranged through an online dating service. They have put their information online, including the kind of person they'd be interested in meeting, and you've responded to this or vice versa. Is this really any different to responding to a job advertisement? You have been matched by the values, interests and experience you are looking to gain from your new relationship with an employer. The challenge you are faced with is getting them to believe that you are a suitable employee. The dating process follows a very similar pattern.

---

[1] CV stands for 'Curriculum Vitae' – the European name for Résumé. For simplicity, I'll be using CV throughout this book

Image

From the time that you meet your potential employer in the waiting area / lobby / reception etc. you are being judged. The employer is working out in their mind whether you seem like the kind of person they want to work with. Effectively: are *you* the person they are looking for? They are assessing everything about your image and the way you present yourself:

Here's a list of things to consider:

Image

- Your smile
- Eye Contact
- Personal Grooming
- Clothing / Attire
- Engagement
- Body Language
- Warmth
- Speech: Volume, Clarity & Tone
- Self Confidence

What is the perception of the person meeting you?

Whenever you meet anyone; see someone just walking in a street, a shop, a restaurant, you start to form an opinion about that person – really quickly. It is no different when attending an interview. We naturally look at everyone's appearance, grooming, manner etc and start to compute the messages they are sending through their body language. We look for signs of engagement with us through their eye contact, tone of voice and gestures. And all of this happens within the first 2 or 3 minutes. In psychology this is called the 'cognitive unconscious'. An easier explanation is: 'first impressions count'.

Finding a balance in the way you present yourself is difficult if you are unaccustomed to interviews. Overdoing it could give the impression that you are insincere or fake; under-do it and you could appear cold, disengaged or aloof. Non-verbal communication is just as important as verbal. If you cross your arms, sit back in your chair and frown, what impression are you putting forth? Contrast that with someone bouncing about in their chair with wild, excited eyes! Who wants to work with someone like that? The best sales people automatically mirror the person they are selling to. This chameleon-like approach means they are effective communicators to whoever they encounter regardless of their age, status or the formality of the occasion. So try to judge the way your interviewer is coming across and engage with them in a similar manner.

Engagement, warmth and self-confidence are incredibly important. Interviews are not beauty contests but if you come across as a warm, enthusiastic, interested and engaging individual, people will often overlook any perceived weakness, because you seem like such a nice, capable person. A lot of this comes from your self-confidence and how you portray yourself. For many, coming across with self-confidence is not easily achieved. However, if you practice a lot of the information in this book and really think about how to develop relationships, your confidence will increase. Just like putting on a great suit or a pretty dress, your self-confidence will increase if you practice what to say and know what *not* to say.

Without any doubt, all of this will be noticed by the interviewer.

Personal Grooming & Your Attire

Many companies use an 'applicant interview form' that the interviewer will fill in during the interview. There is almost always a section about the personal presentation of the applicant. Visible tattoos, ear-rings and piercings, nail polish, sideburns / beards, hairstyle, make-up and finally your attire will all be assessed. It may be stating the obvious but the following checklist should be considered before attending an interview.

Men:

- Conservative, dry-cleaned suit: black, navy or charcoal grey.
- White, long-sleeved dress shirt (avoid button-down)
- Conservative silk tie, coordinated with suit (avoid thin fashion ties or bulky knots)
- Dark socks – black, dark grey or dark blue.   Avoid novelty socks!
- Polished leather business shoes: black (avoid brown)
- Belt: black
- Minimal or no jewellery – no ear-rings or facial piercings.
- Neat, professional hairstyle
- Clean-shaven or neatly trimmed facial hair
- Avoid strong aftershave and/or cologne
- Clean and neatly trimmed fingernails

Women:

- Solid, dark colour, dry cleaned & conservative suit – skirt-suits are considered more professional than trouser-suits; skirt length should be at least to the knee
- White or light coloured shirt – avoid low-cut necklines and busy patterns
- Conservative shoes: moderate heel, closed toe, coordinated with suit.
- Limited, conservative jewellery – no facial piercings
- Neat, professional hairstyle
- Neutral tights – bring an extra pair just in case
- Light make-up and perfume
- Clean and neatly trimmed fingernails
- Small handbag or briefcase
- Portfolio with a pen, paper and extra copies of your CV

Check the company out thoroughly, even to the point of looking at the employees going in and out of the building. Do you present yourself in a similar way to them?

It is important to note that if the company has a dress-down policy, you should still turn up in a suit for the interview. Never attend and interview in dress-down attire unless you have been formally notified that this is ok.

The Pitch

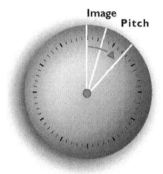

So now you've been greeted in reception and you've been invited into the meeting room to start the interview. After a short period of small talk, the interviewer will find an appropriate moment to make it clear that the interview will now begin. It will typically sound a bit like this:

> *"Thanks for coming in to meet with me today. Perhaps we could start by you telling me a bit about your background and then we can walk through the role and your experience in more depth. Afterward, I'm sure you have some questions for me, so we'll see where that takes us."*

This is typical of many interviews - but what they are really saying is: *'Ok, you've got about an hour of my time; pitch me the reason for hiring you?'* In other words: What makes you a strong candidate for this role?

Sales people know that within the first 30 seconds of speaking to a customer over the phone, they have got to deliver a strong and relevant sales message about their product or they will lose their customer's interest. So they work very hard to hone their delivery to a quick, attention-grabbing pitch that nets results.

At a job interview, you are the product on sale – focus on being able to sell that product well!

In pitching for a job, you have to get across to the interviewer that you have done your homework. So your pitch must include a message that answers the following questions:

1. **What do you know about the company?**
2. **What do you know about the job?**
3. **Why are you here?**

It doesn't matter if it is the Apple Corporation, General Motors or D'Amico's Coffee Shop, if you can't answer these questions, you might as turn around and walk out. Very few employers would warm to a candidate who didn't know about the company, the job or why they have turned up for the interview.

1. What do you know about the Company?

You will not be expected to know everything about the company but at the very least you should research the following:

- **Website:** (company history, senior board members, products and services offered by the company, geographical coverage and office locations). Check this out in detail.
- **Specialisation:** What separates the company from their competitors? How are they perceived by the market they operate in?

- **Management:** Who runs the company? Who is your interviewer? (Linked In, Xing profile etc.) What are their backgrounds?
- **Financial position:** There are hundreds of sources available for this information; a quick check on an internet search engine should produce enough information to satisfy you. The share price, company trading reports, market analysis etc., are all very useful.
- **The Press:** What is the press saying about the company?

Here is a real life example:

A candidate I worked with recently attended an interview with a huge company that was embroiled in a highly publicised court case. Senior Management were being interviewed in the USA and in the UK by government committees regarding their behaviour in the run-up to the court case. The interviewer asked the candidate what she thought about the situation: unfortunately she didn't know anything about it. Result? No job.

I despair when I learn that a candidate I'm representing has not prepared properly for an interview. Particularly as I had spent time going through her interview preparation with her and had emphasised the importance of gaining topical knowledge of the company prior to the interview – inclusive of the pending court case.

The client was particularly disappointed because on paper, she was the perfect candidate. However, if she didn't know anything about the court case and the products and services the company offers, it was apparent that she'd conducted minimal research on the firm. If she couldn't be bothered to research the company, they would not take her forward through the interview process.

Imagine turning up at an interview with Disney and not knowing a single movie they've made? Microsoft, without knowing who the founder is? Coca Cola without knowing where the headquarters are based? Siemens without knowing their product lines? I know this sounds patronising but it is essential that you research the company you are interviewing for thoroughly. You will then have a lot of topical information to share with them about their business and the market they operate in, making you sound like a very credible candidate. You also appear as though you would really like to work for the company because you know so much about them!

What do you know about the Job?

As a starting point, you need to consider the following carefully:

- Have you read the job description thoroughly?
- Do you have a strong understanding of what the job entails and feel confident you could undertake the role from day one?
- Are there any elements of the job that you have never undertaken? If so, what are they?
- Is there jargon or acronyms being used that you don't understand? (This happens a lot – do a quick Google search on the terms used and you should get the answers you need)

If you haven't looked into these things, then again, you might as well pack up and try somewhere else. The next person they interview will have done their research, will have thought about it more and will perform better than you in the interview.

3. Why are you here?

This is a huge question and one that is highly unlikely anyone will ever ask you directly. But I promise you, it is going through the mind of the interviewer.

If you have not thought about this question in advance of your interview – there is a very high percentage chance that you will be unsuccessful.

There are hundreds of individual reasons that prompt people to look for a new job: the commute is a nightmare; there is no career progression; the company is in a difficult financial position; you haven't had an increase in pay in 3 years etc. All of these are valid reasons to move on but they are not the best reason for leaving your current employer. The best reason for leaving your current job is because you would like to do the job that you are interviewing for.

What employers want to hear is that their role sounds like it is very closely aligned to your career interests. Having researched the company and the job description, it seems to be exactly the kind of opportunity that you would like to take on. Then you can add extras like the commute to your current job is a nightmare. Employers are selfish. They want to hear that you were sold on the job as soon as you heard about it.

There is nothing worse than interviewing someone who cannot explain why they are interested in the position and joining the company. What is prompting the decision to leave your current firm in favour of this job? If you are able to start the job immediately, then there will be some explaining to do regarding why you are not working at the moment (see the appendix on redundancy or being fired). Ultimately, if you give the interviewer the impression that you are just looking for a job, any job; you will drop to the bottom of their list.

Take some time to think about why you are attending this interview. What interests you about this role and why? What makes you want to leave your current job in favour of this role?

Create your own list that could be based on the following factors and more:

- Better firm (larger/ smaller/ more dynamic/ market share/ reputation/ start-up)
- More responsibility: a bigger challenge, larger team to manage /smaller team to manage, more focused / less focused on a particular job function
- Career progression: opportunities available across the business
- Location: closer to home, easier commute.
- More rewarding: better pay, better benefits such as pension scheme, bonus potential
- Culture of the organisation: social responsibility / learning & development / training / community
- Hours: Work / Life balance, shift patterns, flexibility

Beware: In a general sense, switching jobs just for a pay increase cannot be the only reason you give for leaving your current job. It is a factor but not the sole reason otherwise you run the risk of being greedy.

The 2-4 minute Pitch

So now that you have a good understanding of the components of a pitch, you can demonstrate quickly that you know about:

- The Company
- The Job
- Why you are here for an interview?

Here is an example of how to put it all together:

The candidate is applying to be the Operations Director for a new chain of Coffee Shops that have plans to expand nationally very quickly.

'You can see from my CV that I attended University and studied the History of Art, it's a fascinating course and I loved it, but the vocational opportunities from that type of degree are somewhat limited.

I worked at The American Coffee Company during my degree and after I finished University, they promoted me to manage a shop. This led to becoming a Store Trainer, where I helped to open other branches and train new staff. I loved the role but after 3 years, I wanted to do something more challenging. I joined Coast to Coast Coffee where I became Area Manager covering 15 shops. Because of my training background, I was able to implement a series of changes that improved profitability in my region by over 15%. This led to a promotion the following year to take up the role of Regional Manager. We've been able to achieve a lot with a focus on quality and training. I love the role but feel that I need to keep challenging myself because I've been with the firm for 6 years and unless my boss quits, I can't really go much further.

I was particularly interested in this role when I saw it advertised. I want to be part of a new and vibrant business and think I can bring a lot of experience in relation to your plans to open multiple sites quickly. I like the concept of the company and think you have a pretty clear vision of where you'd like to be in the marketplace.'

This pitch is warm but not over the top. It doesn't say I'm the best candidate in the world but it does have a chronological history of achievement and progression. It also highlights some specific job-relevant skills that this new job will require. It would be received well.

Here is another for a student applying for a job in Sales at a Book Store.

I finished school last month and have just come back from a holiday in Italy with two of my friends. I'm looking for a job and I saw the ad for this one and wanted to apply right away. I have come in this shop many times and always liked the atmosphere. The staff seem to be really friendly and whenever you have a question, they seem to know exactly what you're looking for. I don't have much experience - I worked at the Cinema last summer in the ticket sales office - but I do think I could learn quickly. I don't have any other commitments at the moment so could work pretty well whenever you needed.

This pitch is more about saying: I have no experience but I do have a strong understanding of what is required and could fit in well with the culture. It also expresses a willingness to learn and respect for the people already working at the firm. It also seems honest.

Final Note on the Pitch:

No matter what the job, in the first 10 minutes of interviewing someone, if the applicant does not seem to have conducted research into the company, hasn't thought about the job and can't explain why they were drawn to the role, it is very unlikely they will be selected.

Validation

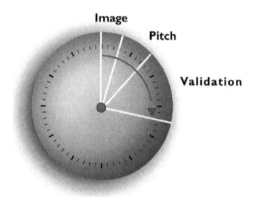

Let's go back to the time that the Employer first found out about you. They saw your CV, maybe read a brief about you from the recruiter; you might have written a great cover letter or formatted your CV in a way that gets the reader's attention. Whatever you did, you've made it to the interview and hopefully will meet the expectations of the person who invited you to meet with them: the Employer.

As they observe and listen to you through the Image and Pitch phases, they are rapidly computing the criteria for the role against your candidacy. So they start to ask questions about who you are; about your experience, the depth of your knowledge, the way you communicate etc. In short, they begin *validating* the preconceived ideas they had about you when they first saw your CV.

The Validation phase is where employers ask questions that are specific to your experience, finding out whether you have the skills to take on the role. But in reality, what this boils down to is that they are really assessing where your strengths and weaknesses lie.

What are your Strengths and Weaknesses?

Very few employers will ever ask this question directly. Instead they come up with devious ways to ask the same question:

Q1: 'If I were to call your last employer, what would he or she tell me about you?'

Q2: 'In your last appraisal, what were the personal development points that they asked you to work on?'

Q3: "What do you think you could bring to the role? What challenges would you face?"

These questions enable the interviewer to root out where you may be lacking. Once you respond, they then have something to probe even further, i.e.:

Here is an answer to the first question that someone recently told me:

"I think my boss would say that he's sorry to see me go. I think he'd say I was hard-working but I can get bored easily. He knows I didn't like the administration side of things there so he'd probably mention that. Overall though, I was there longer than most people so I don't think he'd say I was terrible or anything. I mean, I'm pretty sure he liked me."

An answer like this, gives the interviewer a huge amount of information about you – most of it is **not** good.

- Here are a few of the assumptions they could draw from that response:
- Possible relationship problems with your boss: perceived distance or lack of interaction with him, lack of understanding between you.
- You get bored easily but did the job anyway: How do you pride yourself on your work? Are you just going through the motions? What is the quality of your work like? If you're bored, why didn't you look for another job? Why did you take a job that sounded boring? What is your ambition?
- You don't like administration. This speaks volumes about you. No one likes tedious administrative work yet if the job is office based, you will have administrative responsibilities, whether you like it or not. If you hated admin, why did you do the job? What if the job you're applying for has admin involved? Why would anyone hire you if it did?
- You stuck the job out longer than most people. So what was wrong with the job? Why were people leaving? Couldn't you and your colleagues work to change the place? Didn't you have a voice? If your boss was that bad, why didn't you leave a long time before hand?

I am exaggerating the point somewhat but I am sure you can see that the employer could make assumptions that could count against you. If anything, an answer like the one above casts doubt about your candidacy.

Why you must know your Strengths and Weaknesses

Knowing your strengths and weaknesses isn't just about creating a list of bullet points that you can list off from memory. They are **tools** to help you respond well to probing questions about you and your experience.

Here is a common set of responses to the question "What are your strengths and weaknesses?"

Strengths	Weaknesses
Team-player	Take too much on
Hardworking	Get bored easily
Organised	Get frustrated by delays
Efficient	Sometimes pay too much attention to detail
Friendly	
Good communicator	
Attention to detail	

The X Factor Moment

Everyone knows the X Factor TV program. Like it or loathe it, the format has huge numbers of people lining up to display their talents in front of a panel of judges. They have 2 minutes to impress them or they're finished. This principle is very similar for interviews – here's why:

Think about the common list of strengths and weaknesses on the previous page and then answer this question:

Q: If 1000 people were going for this job, how many of them would say the same thing?

A: Almost everyone.

Why would anyone give responses that are the same as everyone else? To be the stellar candidate, your responses have got to stand out from the crowd. If this was the X Factor, would your list of strengths get you through to the next round? Cheesy as this may seem, it does make sense.

Now answer this question:

Q: If you listed the previous examples as your strengths and weaknesses, is there a possibility that the interviewer could come to the conclusion that some of these responses sound rehearsed?

A: Yes, definitely.

People stay up all night to memorise their list of strengths and weaknesses without realising that they sound like they have rehearsed the whole thing when the time comes. What is the point of memorising something that makes you sound average at best?

Consider the following common statement:

'If you don't know your own strengths and weaknesses, you don't know how to sell yourself.'

Everyone knows this. But how do I articulate myself in a way that stands out from the crowd and doesn't sound rehearsed? The answer is to know what every employer always looks for in assessing an applicant.

Strengths

My Eureka Moment!

In 2003, a candidate applied for a job I'd advertised and sent me both his CV as well as his most recent Employee Appraisal – he was working for a major investment bank and his appraisal was very impressive. (I should note that it is extremely rare for anyone to send through their appraisal so I'd printed it off as I was intrigued by the questions asked). Two weeks later, another candidate, this time working at a major accounting firm, did the same thing. Weirdly, both appraisal forms looked almost identical, asking exactly the same questions! (In all my time in recruitment, I've only ever been sent 3 people's appraisal form – two of them came within 2 weeks of each other).

Both appraisals asked the candidate to fill in a self-assessment based on a series of questions under the following headings:

1. **People Skills**
2. **Client Focus**
3. **Commercial Awareness**
4. **Technical / Operational Effectiveness**
5. **Influence**
6. **Motivation**

My eureka moment came along when it dawned on me that if a major investment bank and a major accounting firm asked the same of their people in an appraisal, then all my candidates would need to do is *make the 6 points their strengths* at an interview and they could truly stand out. After all, they would be telling the interviewer precisely what every professional employer looks for in every individual they hire, and then appraise, them on every 6 months. Think about it: Lawyers, Doctors, Accountants, Scientists, Business Managers, Salespeople etc. will all be expected to demonstrate their competencies in these 6 areas.

Years on, I have reviewed literally thousands of job descriptions. In every one of them, the request is for people who can demonstrate competency in a range of areas that always boil down to these 6 critical areas. The words they use may be different but I promise you, they all arrive at the same thing. You may already possess a few job descriptions. Have a look at them and you'll start to see that the criteria they set will somehow incorporate these 6 points almost every time.

In short, these are the 6 competencies that every single employer in the country looks for in assessing job applicants. Once hired, the employer will then evaluate the employee's performance in these areas too.

So how do you pull all of this together?

Let's evaluate each of these competencies in turn.

People Skills

This is an opportunity to explain how you positively interact with others. Any of the following attributes would come under the people skills subject area:

Teamwork, leadership, coaching and training, personal organisation, communication (to your boss, to subordinates, to clients and customers), people management, project management and coordination, the ability to build relationships etc...

Think about how you interact with others in each of the areas above but more importantly, how do you interact with people who are difficult? What challenges do you face when it comes to working with others? This will be tested during the interview process. You should be able to give examples of strength in the way you positively interact with others using the attributes above and more. How you've used your People Skills to manage both good and challenging relationships.

Client Focus:

Your clients are the people you support at work as well as your customers, and this is all about providing good service. How do you anticipate the needs of your clients before they even ask for assistance?

I use the analogy of a waiter in a restaurant who clears, pours and delivers without interrupting the conversation – whatever I need is delivered promptly and efficiently without fuss. When I want something, he/she is there immediately, listening to me and offering suggestions based on what I've said or asked for. Translate that into any job and you can see that is what makes a great employee.

Are you continually striving to improve the services that your clients are paying you for? If so, how?

Commercial Awareness

How much do you know about the market your company operates in? Do you read the relevant press and or trade news to keep up to speed? If you're in Marketing, do you read Marketing Week?

Keeping abreast of trends in the industry you operate in, will demonstrate that you have a vested interest in the job you perform. It's not all about the pay-cheque!

If you have never read the trade press or the financial news, you would be amazed how much you can pick up in grabbing the latest edition of the Economist, the Financial Times or an industry relevant journal like a Marketing Week, Design Week or other trade-relevant publication. Diving in and grabbing the headlines will make you sound far more knowledgeable than if you've never bothered before and it will be topical information you can bring into the conversation with your interviewer.

At the bare minimum, read the business, financial or trade-press regularly. If you don't, you can expect the employer to think that you don't really care about the welfare of the business or industry they operate in. A technical business sample question could be: If the government and central bank demanded a 1% rise in interest rates, how would that impact our economy? What would it do to business? Who would it affect? Would anyone benefit?

People who use their market knowledge to bring about improvements are always highly valued.

Technical / Operational Effectiveness

You have been trained or educated to achieve a high degree of technical and operational expertise. Can you give examples of how you put these skills into action within your job? What skills do you have that you are an expert in or perform to a higher standard than your peers?

Do you think about improvements to systems, processes, procedures, company policies etc and put them into action? Can you cite examples of where your technical skills or operational abilities really improved the business?

Influence

If there is a single bullet point that employers look for in a hire, it is their ability to influence others in a positive way. Can you bring about improvement or change with apparent ease and gain the backing of your peers on initiatives you present? Your ideas, adopted by the team, become *team ideas* that take root and grow into a wholesale process improvement. Great leaders seize on good ideas and then coordinate the team to implement the change, crediting those for a job well done.

People who have the ability to affect, control or manipulate something or someone in a positive way are an extremely valuable resource to a progressive organisation.

All effective leaders have this quality. Do you have examples of when you used your influencing capabilities to change things such as conduct, thoughts or decisions within your current job? This skill is what can really set you apart from other job candidates.

Having the ability to influence doesn't always mean you have to be a 'people-leader' or a 'captain of industry'. It simply means that when you speak, people will listen to your ideas and value your input. It can be small things that make wholesale changes on the profitability of a company. The person who said: 'I've been thinking, what if we just tried it like this, we could save a fortune...' can have a fantastic influence on the business. Conversely, the person who complains all the time has a negative influence that over long periods of time can be very damaging.

What influence have you had in your last job that really impacted the way you and your colleagues operate?

Motivation

What gets you out of bed every day to perform this job?

If you're attending a job interview, you need to be able to demonstrate an enthusiasm for the job you're being considered for. You are motivated by the opportunity. You are ambitious and willing to put in all the hours necessary to fulfil your obligations.

Good employers think about planning for the future, known as succession planning. Your motivation and ambition should be on display such that they begin thinking from the outset: 'If this person is as good as I think they are, we may have a business leader of the future on our hands!' I am not kidding, they do actually think about these things right away.

Articulating your Strengths

The subtlety of the interview process means that it would be an extraordinary coincidence if someone started asking you for a précis on each of the 6 competencies. However they will ask questions that fall under these categories. (See the appendix – Competency Based Questions).

But the key to good interview preparation is to spend time considering your strengths in each of the 6 competencies and then being able to call upon them effortlessly during a discussion. It becomes the natural manner in the way you explain your expertise, not a list you've spent the night memorising!

Here they are again:

1. **People Skills**
2. **Client Focus**
3. **Commercial Awareness**
4. **Technical / Operational Effectiveness**
5. **Influence**
6. **Motivation**

By now, if you've thought about it, you should already have some great ideas that you could bring into an interview that are far better than the responses that most people give in relation to their strengths. So what about the weakness?

Weaknesses

No one likes having to admit their weaknesses. Admitting you're not particularly good at one facet of your job or that one characteristic of your personality could do with some re-tuning is uncomfortable for almost everyone. We do not like to feel vulnerable which is at the heart of our basic list of emotions under the heading: Fear.

So how can you give a response that is **bullet-proof** and will impress your prospective employer?

Let's look at the responses we gave earlier. It is very common for people to reel off honest responses like those below when asked what their weaknesses are:

Weaknesses
Take too much on
Get bored easily
Get frustrated by delays
Sometimes pay too much attention to detail

But what is the employer's perception of these responses?

Weaknesses	Employers Perception
Take too much on	Can't delegate – afraid to ask for help
Get bored easily	Might hate our job – lots of admin
Get frustrated by delays	Likely to be high maintenance – won't assimilate in our bureaucratic culture
Sometimes pay too much attention to detail	Would take too long to get anything done – would need micro-managing

The employer may read into what you are telling them with a completely different interpretation and what is worse, jot it down as an indelible reminder of this perception. They will then pass their notes on to the next person to interview you for the job, who will immediately base much of their opinion of you on what their colleague has written down! That is only *if* you get to the next stage of the process!

This is why recruitment consultants always tell you to turn a negative response into a positive:

> *'I used to take too much on but over the last year, I've been able to delegate far more efficiently and am conscious that I need to share the workload with my colleagues.'*

This kind of response turns something that could be perceived as a weakness into something you recognise needed improvement and you've since worked hard to ensure that it does not become a problem anymore. The net effect should be that the employer recognises you have worked on improving yourself and lists it as a minor flaw rather than a major weakness.

My problem with 'the turning negative into a positive' approach is that it means someone could admit to almost anything but say they've improved or learned from this and don't let it happen anymore. It can also sound very rehearsed. My advice is to tread carefully in this territory. (See the C.A.R.L approach in the appendix).

The Bullet Proof Weakness

'Experience: there is always something new to learn'.

Even those who are the best in the world at a particular skill will tell you they are always trying to improve. They want to be the best, so they are always working on particular facets of their skill-set to maintain the highest possible standards. You don't have to be the world's best in anything to reference the exact same thing.

> *"I am good at my job and I am always looking to improve. I will only get better by working hard and gaining more experience."*

How many sportsmen or women have you heard say something like this after they have just competed? It is almost their mantra. Think about it, the best sports-people have experience, they can handle the pressure, they are leaders, they are the people that are top of their game but still know that they can improve.

Back to the real world:

If an employer asked the direct question: "What are your weaknesses?" Here is the kind of response that is truthful without giving away a particular issue that could count against you:

> *'I suppose my biggest weakness would be that I only have 4 years of experience in this field and I know I still have a lot to learn. I think that's what draws me to this role, because I know I can specialise more in an area that I'm keen to continue learning about.'*

> *'Yes but surely you have other weaknesses?'*

> *'Well yes, if you go through every part of my current job there are long lists of things I can improve on. But I put almost all of this down to the fact I need to continue to learn and develop my skills through more experience. I think, for my level, I am good with people; my clients seem to like me a lot. I'm passionate about what I do because my career is very important to me. Generally, I think I perform my job to a high standard but I am not the finished article and know I can improve.'*

This is a natural way to reference that the one and only weakness the individual has is their experience. The employer will be satisfied with this answer because it is honest and sounds completely genuine. They already know that with 4 years of experience, the candidate is nowhere near perfect – but that is ok, because the employer is not looking for someone with only 4 years of experience who can run the company! They are looking for someone with 4 years behind them, possibly more, who can do the job on offer. Why would the employer waste their time interviewing someone if they didn't think they could do the job on review of the candidate's CV?

Here is your new mantra in relation to your weakness:

'Experience: there is always something new to learn'.

You don't have to use these exact words, but if you remember them as reference for your lack of experience, you will have a bullet proof response.

Weakness & the 80:20 Principle

Bear with me, this will make sense!

Viliford Pareto was an Italian economist, philosopher and political scientist who observed that 80% of the land in Italy was owned by only 20% of the population. It then followed that 80% of the wealth of the country was held by 20% of the population. This ratio still holds today.

Management Science began as a subject of study in the last century and has grown exponentially. Business leaders realised that Pareto's formula could be utilised in many different ways: 80% of a company's sales came from 20% of their client base; 20% of their stock on sale took up 80% of their warehouse. In project management, the first 10% of a project and the last 10% take up 80% of the time devoted to the total project's work hours. The 80:20 principle can be translated into many other situations and is regularly cited in the study of management science.

So what has this got to do with Weaknesses in a job interview?

One of the strongest reasons that people generally have when switching jobs is that the new opportunity offers a challenge they are not getting in their current job. When job-seeking, you target the jobs that you feel you have the right level of experience to cover a large percentage of the job as advertised. So the 80:20 principle applies because:

80% is what you can do

20% is the challenge

You feel confident you can do 80% of the job well. Your experience has covered this. But there is an element of this new job that you haven't covered and that is your challenge. *Your challenge is your **only** perceived weakness.*

Think about it. If you felt that you could do 90% of the job without question, would you really want to take the job? If it was 100%? Most people agree that there is no point taking on a job when there is very little challenge in it - even if they are offering an increase in pay. It would be better to hold out for something else.

The alternative viewpoint would be if you felt you could only really cover 60% of the job and 40% would be the challenge. To most, they would simply turn it down as being too big to take on. Why leave my job to be dropped in at the deep end with a high percentage chance of failing?

People strike a happy balance when they can do 80% of the job effortlessly and will be able to learn the other 20% as they go on. Employers also want people who recognise that they will have a challenge ahead of them. The challenge will keep the employee motivated keep the recruit motivated for some time. If you were the boss, would you realistically hire someone who is likely to be bored within a short period of time or someone who really wants to learn?

Another way of looking at this is:

80% is what you can do = **Your Strengths**

20% is your challenge = **Your Weakness**

How to use the 80:20 Principle during an Interview

As mentioned earlier, the one and only weakness you should ever refer to is a lack of experience. But we know that employers are clever in the way that they ask questions about you. So if we refer to the question asked earlier:

"In your last appraisal, what were the areas for development that you were asked to focus on?"

The first thing you should know is that the interviewer will never get their hands on your last appraisal so you do not need to divulge anything negative that might have been discussed. The second thing is that if you do divulge something that needs fixing, you are giving the interviewer a reason not to hire you. I am not saying you should lie; far from it. But you do not need to tell anyone that one of the reasons you are leaving your current job is because you pathologically hate one of your colleagues!

So your answer could be:

'Well the last appraisal was almost a year ago and we discussed many issues related to my job and performance - how I interact with others, my work habits and application, my career goals etc. Virtually all of it was positive but if I'm honest, I needed to take on more responsibility if I was going to get promoted and we both recognised that. I took on the management of one member of the team and now I manage a team of 5 people which is great. If I look back on that discussion, I think I have come a long way in managing people and taking on further responsibility for the

business. I needed to take on more challenges, I did this and now I'm looking for a new one. '

If the job you are applying for has new challenges within it, think of your lack of experience as being a constituent part of what makes up your own 20% in the 80:20 ratio. Every time you find yourself saying 'Uh no, I've no experience of that' then, where possible, try and turn that into 'but that's why I'm interested in this role, because I want to take on this kind of challenge'.

If they've read through your CV, they should already know that you are likely to be missing one or two elements of the criteria they require.

The 80:20 Principle in Real Life

In 2013, Angela Ahrendts, the highly successful CEO of Burberry, the global fashion business, resigned her position to take over as a Senior Vice President at Apple. The financial press were shocked and Burberry's share price dropped considerably in reaction to the news. But why would Apple hire someone from the fashion industry? She has no clue about consumer electronics!

Clearly, it was because she has the requisite retail experience and knows how to gain and grip consumer interest. Her challenge is that she needs to learn all about Apple products and what will sustain their appeal to consumers. In effect, the 80% that she can do is all about brand building and retail management. The 20% challenge is that she needs to understand the culture of Apple and what makes Apple consumers tick.

Recap on the Validation Phase

Earlier we discussed the weaknesses we used earlier and ask the same question again:

'In your last appraisal, what were the areas for development that you were asked to focus on?'

And you listed these as the areas you needed to work on:

Weaknesses
Take too much on
Get bored easily
Get frustrated by delays
Sometimes pay too much attention to detail

I think you can see that with each one, you are building a set of reasons for them to hire someone else!

The Validation Phase that employers typically use to draw out the strength or weakness of your experience is clearly a very critical phase in the structure and process of an interview. To me, it is the defining phase on whether you will be successful or not. This is why it is critical to have a strong command of your strengths and weaknesses.

The 15-20 Minute Rule

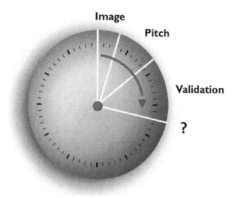

Earlier, I mentioned Social Conditioning, which is like a software program that runs in all of us and determines the way we build relationships with each other. The software processes the signals, styles and mannerisms we acknowledge or receive from whoever we encounter and then runs this against a pre-coded list of preferences we have. We do this constantly – it is the *cognitive unconscious* in operation. It sits at the very core of our brains and is all based on emotion. In order for you and the other person to get along, our pre-coded lists of preferences need to be similar.

Now compare this same process to speed-dating. Would you go out with someone who presents themselves poorly, can't really talk about themselves in a clear and confident way and can't really outline any of their redeeming qualities? Most of us would say no. After 15 minutes talking to this person, you would have a pretty clear idea that they were not for you.

So if your interviewer is not getting the right message within the first 15-20 minutes of meeting you, you are very unlikely to be able to change their overall impression.

The great thing about this is that we all operate on different levels. Mathematicians don't tend to hang out with liberal arts people. Football players don't tend to date scientists. We find our jobs and our friends based on our own set of social criteria, interests and abilities. You and your interviewer share a common interest in the job you're being interviewed for.

You applied for the job because you feel it meets the criteria you set for the job you want to do. Your interviewer reviewed your CV and invited you in for an interview. After assessing your personal presentation, your interest in this field and the answers you gave to questions he/she has about your experience, they will have formed an opinion. Hopefully, it will be that you are the right person for the job!

If not, they begin to shut down. Generally this is done slowly. Employers feel duty bound to give you a chance, even if they know in their hearts you haven't got a chance and haven't had one since the opening minutes of the interview. Most people don't want to appear rude so they go through the motions. You could get a response like:

'Well thanks for coming in, we have a number of people to see this week and will be letting people know our shortlist at the end of the week.'

If they really like you, they will be telling you something far more positive. They will confirm their interest in you by telling you they would like you to meet more people in the company.

The 15-20 minute rule is a silent marker that everyone in the world uses as a determinant in the way they build relationships. Think about the last time you were at a party and chatting with someone you'd never met before. Within a few minutes you found that they were not your kind of person. Rather than be rude, you make a polite excuse to say you were meant to be getting a drink for someone. Employers do exactly the same thing – they shut down and try to close out the conversation quickly.

If an employer likes what they are hearing at the 15-20 minute point, the dynamic of the interview begins to change. They become more relaxed, possibly friendlier and they begin **selling** the job to you. After all, they brought you in for an interview and if they like what they've been hearing, why wouldn't they begin convincing you that you could have a great career with them. From then on, you need to align yourself firmly to their vision of the ideal candidate and enjoy the conversation.

Alignment

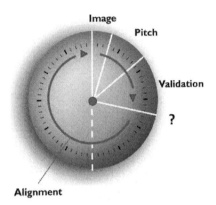

Most employers I speak to, have a pretty good idea of the kind of person they are likely to meet, just from reading the individual's CV. This could be drawn from the University the individual attended, the shop they worked in, the architectural design company they worked for, their sporting interests, their personal achievements.

Whatever preconceptions they have of you as a candidate, your focus on meeting them is to align yourself to their interests. There is no point attending an interview with a long list of things you expect from them. It is their job to offer you.

So many candidates I speak to, screw up interviews because they are not considering what the employer wants; they are only thinking about what they want. This is a fundamental error. You responded to their job advertisement or you were contacted by a recruiter on their behalf about the job. The employer wants to meet someone who is similar to their vision of the ideal candidate; more importantly, someone who is aligned to their way of thinking.

Again this comes down to your pre-interview preparation; your familiarity with the company, with the job they are recruiting for and why you want to do it. The more thought you've put into it, the more credible you will come across.

Consider the best interview you've ever had with someone you've never met before. In most cases, they were smiling at you quite early on, asking questions you could easily answer and generally nodding in agreement with the things you said. That is alignment. Consider a great first date you went on with someone you didn't know well, the same thing happened. You had an easy, friendly conversation that flowed along effortlessly. It just felt very comfortable. That is also alignment. These are examples of how relationships are developed.

As I mentioned in the 15-20 Minute rule section, if an employer has arrived at the opinion that you are not right for their role, they will begin to shut down and go through the motions to close out the interview. However, if they like you, you can actually see them start *selling* the job to you; making it clear they have an interest in you as a candidate.

Here are a few examples of the 'buying signs' that employers may display:

- Inviting other people in to meet you. 'I'd like you to meet Steve, our Head of Department. How are you doing for time?'
- Body language switches from formal to informal. Displays signs of interest in the conversation.
- Asks about your availability and notice period. Are there any issues you anticipate in leaving your current employer?
- Comments about particular elements of your experience with approval.

- Tells you they would like you to come back the following week to meet more of the team.
- Asks you what your notice period is.

Alignment is best maintained by finding common interests. Given that the employer expects you to have an interest in the job on offer, it stands to reason that the more you are aligned to what they are looking for, the better your chance of being successful.

The Alignment phase is what cements a new relationship. In the context of an interview, it is what will affirm in the mind of the interviewer that you are the right person for the job.

Ensuring Alignment

The nerve-wracking element of interviewing is not knowing what to expect. You have no idea what the person will be like that you are meeting. That's why preparing for interviews is so important: it will put you on as firm a footing as possible.

Do your homework: Who is interviewing you? What is their background? Check them out on Linked In, Facebook, Twitter and any other social media websites. What level are they? Gather your intelligence!

Listen: It may seem obvious but you'd be amazed how often people set their own agenda for an interview and barely listen to what the interviewer is saying or asking. Being alert to the interests, goals and ideas of your interviewer makes alignment so much easier.

Prepare questions: Read the job description or job advertisement and align it to your current experience. There are hundreds of questions about your responsibilities, your accountability, career progression, team size, typical working day or week, volume of output etc. The market the business operates in, the systems they use, the people you'll interact with, their client base and the backgrounds of your potential colleagues are all worth discussing.

Share interests and experience: If you share mutual interests, job experience and seek out opportunities to discuss aligned approaches to solving problems, the conversation will undoubtedly go well.

Be engaging: Your focus is to impress your interviewer and a quick way to do this is to engage with them. Show you are a self-confident, earnest and focused individual who clearly wants the job. Above all, be someone they get the feeling they would enjoy spending 40 hours a week with. Being engaging is a two way street – find a balance that means you share the conversation rather than dominate it.

Final Word on Alignment

Let's assume that you are going for an important job with a market leading company. You won't just meet one person; you'll meet several, including the Managing Director. This could be drawn out over 3 or 4 interviews, possibly more. Each individual will have their own agenda of what they expect in a new hire but with each person you meet, if they like you they will endorse you to the next person in line. It is therefore critical that you align yourself to each person you meet.

3 Universal Hiring Factors

The critical factors behind every hiring decision will always be that the individual demonstrates the following key attributes:

- **Knowledge**: The individual possesses the right amount of understanding to undertake the job
- **Skills**: The individual possesses the right skills
- **Attitude**: The individual displays a positive, enthusiastic approach to the role

Which one is the most important?

The answer is Attitude. The depth of your knowledge or your current skill levels will always be less important than the attitude you have toward your work and everything it entails. It is critical that you are aware of this. You can be taught to improve your knowledge and trained to increase your skill level, but if you have a bad attitude, you will never perform the job well or hold the respect of your colleagues.

If you do not display a positive attitude during your interview, you might as well have stayed at home!

Questions to Ask

I get asked about this all the time: 'What should I be asking the employer at the interview?'

The first answer I always give is: **review the six competencies again:**

- People Skills
- Client Focus
- Commercial Awareness
- Technical / Operational Effectiveness
- Influence
- Motivation

Just reading them again, should start to build a huge number of questions about the firm, the role and the person that they are looking to employ. Under People Skills, you could discuss the various stakeholders the individual would need to be working with; the team size, the reporting lines, the people development programs they run etc. Hundreds of questions emanate from just reviewing the competencies again.

The second answer I give is that the more you review about the company, the job and the criteria they've outlined in their job description, the better armed you'll be with questions. People tend to get very nervous at interviews because they've done very little structured preparation in advance. They have no idea what is going to happen at the interview and worse, they have not helped themselves by doing some simple research on the company in advance.

Finally, use common sense. Going in armed with a notebook full of pre-prepared questions is probably over the top, yet having a few carefully selected questions that are not answered on their website or in the job description I would encourage. Things like career progression, organisational structure, training & development, remuneration (though be very careful with that one), work/life balance etc. are all worth questioning / discussing if not covered during the course of the interview.

Ending the Interview

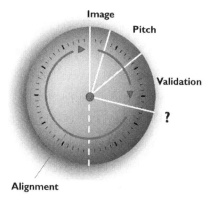

Alignment

Quick recap: The Employer has read through your CV and invited you in for an interview. On meeting you for the first time, they begin assessing the way you present yourself and whether someone like you could fit into the culture of the company. They then ask you to discuss your background i.e.: what's your pitch? Questions follow about how your experience is relevant for the position, and the employer starts to formulate the opinion of whether you are right, or wrong for the role. You have given a very good account of yourself and seem to share the same outlook on why the role is right for you. The overall impression is positive so now what?

Most people leave an interview without gaining an understanding of their position after the interview. Personally, I think you should. But this has to be done tactfully without pushing too hard.

Interviewer: 'Well I think that gives me enough to go on. I have a couple of other people to see this week so I should be able to give you a clearer picture of where we are, early next week.

At this point, most people just say:

> 'Ok thank you, it was a pleasure meeting you. I look forward to hearing from you.'

But it would be better to say something like this:

> 'I understand. I am sure you do have other people to see - it is a great opportunity. Before I go though, I do want you to know that I would be really pleased if I was selected. Based on our discussion today, I know there are a few things I would have to pick up quickly but I would be prepared to work extremely hard to meet my responsibilities. Overall, I am really interested in the job and thanks for taking the time to meet with me.

The word to describe this kind of close to a discussion is: Affirmation.

To seal the deal, you should affirm your interest in the role. Sales people call this 'The Close'. You want to make sure that the Employer is, at the minimum, left with the impression that you are likely to accept the role if they offered it to you. Even if you are not sure if you want the job!

Why? Because if you don't leave a strong, lasting impression, you are simply just one of the people they met in the interview process. You didn't leave them with the impression that you would accept the job in a heartbeat, so there may be a doubt in their mind. *And* it is better to get an offer for a job you don't want than to attend an interview and get nothing out of it. Who knows? The offer might completely change your mind about doing a job you thought you didn't want! If you do want the job, you have made it abundantly clear that you are interested and want to go forward.

Here's another way of looking at it: If you were on a date, would you prefer to hear: *'I'd really like to see you again'* or *'Ok, see ya!'* as a parting comment? You would be left with a much better impression from the first of these statements so: *What does the employer want to hear?*

I also get asked quite often whether it's a good idea to send an email or letter thanking the interviewer for their time. 90% of the time, I would say no. You should have affirmed your interest at the interview. Sending a letter or note can give the impression you are desperate or had to go away and think about your interest in the role. Affirming your interest at the interview has a much stronger impact and leaves a lasting impression on the employer.

I know many people will argue this. Some readers preferring a formal approach may suggest that a follow up letter is a great way to affirm your interest. My opinion is that this is quite weak in today's job world. Face to face communication is so much stronger than any other form of media – use it to its fullest extent. However I will concede that if you applied directly to the firm, then a follow up email or call a week later would be a good idea to keep things moving forward.

Salary Expectations

Typically, the question of what your salary expectation is comes towards the end of the interview. Let the interviewer bring this up rather than you. I strongly advise you to avoid asking questions about salary or employee benefits until the point when you are actually offered the job.

If you are currently working for a competing firm, the interviewer knows that it is unlikely you will move for the same salary as you are on currently – no matter what the circumstances are. So as a general rule, the typical increase you can expect in moving from one job to another is 10% -20%.

Agency Introductions:

If you were put forward by a recruitment agency, then it is best to leave the salary negotiation with the employer to them. Your Recruitment Consultant will have a clear understanding of what the employer is willing to pay for the role and what he/she believes would be possible for you to achieve. They will also advise you on what to say at the interview if you are asked about your salary expectations directly. Also, if you don't like negotiating, let the recruitment agency take what can be an uncomfortable and awkward negotiation process off your hands – this is their expertise. You should also know that the agency will work hard to get you the best salary possible because the more that you get paid, the higher their fee will generally be.

If You've Applied Directly to the Employer

When negotiating for yourself, it's best to tell the employer what you are currently being paid and then wait to see what they offer you. If you are confident in yourself and have interviewed well, it is likely the employer will put a fair and attractive offer to you. They don't want to risk losing you by putting forward an offer that they know you won't accept; that just isn't a good way to start a relationship with an employee. On the other hand, it is highly unlikely that they will double your salary, so it's realistic to expect an offer of between 10% and 20% above your current base. If that doesn't seem to be forthcoming, then simply state that you will consider their offer and let them know.

The Offer

A very important element of negotiating is to avoid disclosing how badly you need or want the job. Expressing you have a strong interest in the role is different to being desperate. It is also a terrible position to begin negotiating from. Play your cards close to your chest but make it obvious you are interested; this is an extension of the alignment phase of the interview process.

When you receive an offer, consider every element of the job – the working hours, the benefits package, the commute, career development and future career prospects. Sometimes, the salary isn't the most important element of the job. Also, consult with your friends, family or colleagues before leaping to a decision – they know you and will give you confidence you are making the right choice.

If you are not satisfied with the offer, be diplomatic. State that their offer does not meet your expectation and back it up with a valid reason. Your expectation needs to be realistic and in line with the market, so it is advisable to look up salary surveys for your area of expertise and location (recruitment companies, web based job-boards and even your own company will have salary bandings for your level). Hopefully they will meet your expectation but if the company refuses to amend or improve their offer, then you have a choice about whether to accept it as it is or not. Do not reject the offer outright; tell them you'll need time to consider it further. This gives you and the employer time to review your respective positions.

Once you verbally accept a job, then the process of sending an employment contract to you will take a few days – normally a week. This buys you some time and gives you the opportunity to think everything through properly. You can, on review of the contract, go back to them and say you'd like elements of their offer to be improved or… you can continue to interview elsewhere. You have only verbally accepted the job; you do not have to sign the contract if you decide to back out.

Assessment Centres

Assessment centres are being used increasingly by companies that are seeking to expand quickly by hiring many people at the same time. They are also used regularly by firms that have Graduate hiring programs every year.

The idea is to create an environment that enables you to demonstrate key workplace skills. So depending on the job, the assessment centre could include any of the following (and more): How you communicate (verbally or in written format); how you work within a team ie: group exercises; assessing your problem-solving skills; how you undertake day to day projects or tasks, and possibly your management or leadership qualities will be put to the test.

Activities that involve brain-storming a problem within a small group and then presenting it to the assessors are common. Individual tasks like role-playing a phone call with a client or customer, or tests that look at the way you prioritise your work are also to be expected.

The most important thing to mention about assessment centres is that you must **participate** in what they ask you to do. Failing to participate or show an interest in the tasks they ask you to perform will mean that the others who do, will progress to the next stage.

You are there to demonstrate how you work well with people and take your work seriously. Like normal interviews, the purpose is to leave the employer with the perception that you are a team-player who performs your job function well and possess an enthusiastic approach to your work.

If you're a Graduate, you will often enter the assessment centre without a real understanding of the role that you are being assessed for. Large firms have a huge array of career paths under one roof, so you may find you are being assessed for a multiple roles within the firm. In this instance, hiring managers actually compete internally for the best talent within the pool of candidates attending. If you participate and perform well during the assessment centre, you could find you have the pick of several job roles to go into rather than just being offered a role they decided that you are best suited to. And this could end up being a role you have less interest in.

Final note: To the despair of many internal recruiters, a huge percentage of exceptionally bright people fail at assessment centres simply because they did not participate like others on the day.

Panel Interviews

Panel interviews are generally used as a way of getting multiple opinions on an individual quickly. They will usually be constructed from people who perform different jobs within the business i.e.: an individual from IT, Legal and Sales could all be there to determine your candidacy.

If you've read through all of the information in this book thoroughly, you should be able to tackle a panel interview just as well as if you were in a one-on-one interview. There is really not much difference but it can be a bit more nerve-wracking walking into a room with a number of people staring back at you. Compose yourself and focus on all the steps we've discussed.

A good tip is to try to understand the angle that each panel member is coming from. Be aware of their job function and how they would interact with you in the job you would be performing.

Appendix

Appendix: A Few of the Basics

Write a Great CV

This book is about Interview Preparation, so it is implied that you've already got the interview and that came from the fact you've written a pretty good CV. However, if you are just entering the job market, I cannot stress how important it is to have a CV that is well formatted and looks professionally presented. If you use Microsoft Office, there are a number of templates that you can use to get started. Do not choose anything too fancy or heavily formatted. (Borders, lots of italics, script-style fonts or wingdings for punctuation are all a bad idea – keep it simple and professional). Whatever you do, make sure you show it to an objective and helpful person for their opinion, before sending it out to anyone. I also have very little faith in people who are CV writers for a living. They tend to produce extremely dull CV's that do little to showcase your strengths and are based on a template that they use for almost everyone. You might as well just use Microsoft Office. Get a friend to show you their version – particularly if it got them a job at a company you respect.

My simple tip would be to try to outline in each job you've done, elements of the 6 key competencies I've outlined in this book. Mentioning your people skills, delivery capability, technical proficiency, business achievements etc will enhance the content of your CV.

Keeping with content, make sure you explain each role you've conducted clearly. Avoid jargon or acronyms that are not in common, everyday use. This may seem harsh but a complete moron should be able to read your CV and fully understand what the function of your job was in each role. If it's not clear, you are asking the interviewer to spend time trying to understand what you did in the job rather than actually interview you.

I will never read everything on a 5 page CV, neither will an employer. For all of you MBA's who are told it is necessary to cram everything onto one page – this is no longer the case and hasn't been for 20 years. A 2-3 page, nicely presented CV is standard.

Your CV is like a passport to getting the job you want. If it is not well written, well formatted and emphasising the strength of your experience, you are already minimising your chance of getting hired.

The Handshake

I feel it's essential to include a note about the importance of the handshake. At the beginning and the end of your meeting, the ceremony of the handshake takes place. Shaking a clammy, sweaty hand is particularly unpleasant. If you are unsure if you suffer from 'clammy hand syndrome', test it out on a trustworthy friend who will provide you with an honest answer. You'd be amazed how easily this can contribute to being a point against you. All that is required is a firm handshake that is neither over-powering nor limp and lifeless.

Focus on the impression you are trying to create?

To be impressive, you need to engage with the interviewer with confidence. No one wants to interview someone who is arrogant, aggressive, aloof, withdrawn, un-engaged etc. They want someone they feel confident can do a good job, meet the criteria for the role and be the kind of person who they can go for a beer with after a long week. Over-ambitious people tend to really irritate interviewers. Balance how you sell yourself with being a genuinely good person to work with. Ultimately, align your personal goals within the context of the job with those of the interviewer.

Notes on Social Media

If you have a page on Facebook, Twitter, Bebo, Myspace or any other social media website, make sure they are all on complete lockdown prior to your interview. You do not want semi-naked pictures of you on a beach in Morocco being passed around ahead of your interview – even if you think you look great! Privacy is key – allowing someone to form anything other than a professional opinion about you is a big mistake and could be very damaging.

For professional networking sites like Linked-In or Xing, post a picture of yourself that is similar to a professional portrait. A picture of you with your kids may seem fine, but it is not giving a professional image to your employer. It is not you in a professional context, which is how they would expect you to appear.

Here is the best description I've seen that nails what employers do **before** you attend an interview. Check out the website of Liz Fosslien at **http://fosslien.com/job/** who provides a funny and irreverent take on the interview process.

you

Google Search   I'm Feeling Lucky

facebook   you   Q

Linked in.   Add Connections

Home   Profile   Inbox   People ▾   you   Q   Advanced

Lock Everything Down!

Competency Based Questions

People live in fear of competency based questions because they are designed to single out how YOU performed a particular task or managed a particular situation. Again this is where some forethought and practice will be beneficial and should quell your fears.

The S.T.A.R. Approach

When providing a response to a competency based question, there is a simple methodology that you should retain that will enable you to give clear and concise answers. It is called S.T.A.R. and is an acronym for Situation, Task, Action & Result. Here is a very typical competency based question:

"Give an example of when you have produced a piece of work for someone that exceeded their expectations?"

Using the STAR approach, you could break your response down in a sequence of steps like this:

> **Situation:** My boss is Managing Director for the UK division of our software business. Globally, there are 24 MD's, 4 Regional Heads and the CEO. Last year, we held the global sales conference in the UK. I was responsible for coordinating the event that we held at Centrepoint in London. Over 90 very senior people were there and it was the first time my boss had been asked to host an event. The last one in London was over 10 years ago.

Task: We needed to put on an impressive event because every year, the conference is held in a different country. So each MD goes out of their way to impress. I chose Centrepoint as the venue because it has a great view of the whole of London.

Action: Working with my boss and a small project team, we coordinated everything from flights and hotels to evening meals in restaurants around the City, as well as a group trip to our manufacturing plant in Bracknell. There was a lot of technical work required as well and I got a number of our senior UK management team on board to help in the planning and sequencing of the event.

Result: We got fantastic feedback from all of the attendees and the CEO praised us on how smoothly everything went. It reflected well on him too. Ultimately, my boss was extremely pleased and kept saying he couldn't have done it without me. I got a good bonus last year because of it.

This is a good example of how a competency based question could be answered. Note that it is brief, explains each step clearly and ends with a positive result. Every response you give should follow a similar pattern. I would urge you to practice giving responses like this to the sample questions on the following pages. It will give you a lot of confidence going into an interview.

The C.A.R.L Approach

There is another acronym called C.A.R.L which can also be applied – this relates to Context, Action, Result and Learning. Context sets the scene of the story, (action and result are the same as STAR) and learning is the knowledge you gained from the experience. This is useful when describing a time that did not go to plan and taught you a valuable lesson.

"Can you describe a time when you let down a client or a colleague. How did you handle the situation?"

This kind of question at an interview can be a killer and needs to be considered carefully.

Using the C.A.R.L approach, the result should end with something like:

> *'…and I would never let that happen again!'*

As one client of mine said recently:

"I don't mind if someone has screwed up in their career. Everyone does. I just hope they don't screw up when they are working for me!"

Learning from your mistakes is obviously very important; just don't admit to making many!

Sample Interview Questions based On the 6 Key Competencies:

As explained in the last section, competency questions should be answered so that they give a clear and concise story behind the situation, the task, and the steps you took to resolve the problem or issue and hopefully achieve a positive result. So use the STAR approach as you practice each question.

- **People Skills:** Teamwork, Leadership, Communication, Organisation, Project Management, Mentoring, Motivating etc. Skills that help achieve shared objectives.
- **Client Focus** - The ability to identify, agree and deliver on client objectives (both internal and external) to ensure client satisfaction and maintain an on-going business relationship.
- **Commercial Awareness** - The ability to harness business/market intelligence and use this knowledge to improve performance and/or adapt to changes in the market place.
- **Technical / Operational Effectiveness** - The ability to plan, implement and deliver solutions that exceed expectations.
- **Influence:** The ability to effect change in a positive, meaningful and lasting manner (possibly the most important competency of them all).
- **Motivation** - Enthusiasm, commitment to and understanding of the role and firm

People Skills:

- How would you describe the effectiveness of your current team? What is your contribution?

- In your career, what has been the most effective team that you have worked in? Why?
- What has been the least effective team you've worked in? Why?
- Tell me about a person you found it difficult to work with. How did you overcome this?
- Have you ever had to give difficult feedback to another member of the team? How did you tackle it?
- Describe a time when you have changed the way you were doing something due to someone else's opinion.
- Can you give examples of when you have trained others? How effective were you?
- What have you done to improve communications / motivation in your team?
- Describe the last time you managed a complaint – either from a customer or a co-worker. How did you handle it?
- If I were to contact your colleagues, what would they tell me about you? What would your boss say?

Employer Perception: The Negative Indicators

- Displays a preference to work alone.
- Takes credit for others work/ideas.
- Lacks empathy toward others
- Unwilling to change or learn from others
- Avoids taking personal responsibility within a team.
- Demonstrates irritation with people.

Client Focus

- Clients can be external (sales related) or internal i.e.: the people you support within the business.
- Can you give me an example of a project where you built a strong relationship with a client? To what do you attribute this success?
- Give an example of when you helped a colleague with a piece of work that generated revenue for the company?
- Give an example of when you have produced a piece of work for someone that exceeded their expectations?
- Can you tell me about the most demanding client that you have worked with? What measures did you take to ensure success?
- Can you give an example of when your technical/industry expertise has been valuable to a client?
- Have you ever had to handle a situation when the client completely changes direction on their brief? How did you handle this?

Employer Perception: The Negative Indicators

- Lacks appreciation of client needs.
- Shows unwillingness to respond to client needs.
- Fails to engage other team-members when necessary
- Misses deadlines.
- Unwilling to adapt to changes in client needs.

Commercial Awareness

- How do you keep your market knowledge up to date? What sources do you use?
- How have you used business knowledge in your work place to improve the services you provide?
- What are the key issues facing the business sector that you work in over the next 5 years? How do you feel these issues should be addressed?
- How have you contributed to making sure that costs are managed in your current role?
- Can you give an example of when you have implemented a commercially successful idea?
- Describe the last time you used your initiative to generate income for the company.
- In your current role how have you developed a network of contacts? How did you use this network to generate business?
- Where do you think your current firm could be more profitable in the marketplace?

Employer Perception: The Negative Indicators

- Has little interest or understanding of the marketplace.
- Does not generate commercially viable ideas.
- Has not used knowledge to commercial advantage.
- Has relevant knowledge, but no evidence of using it to generate opportunities.
- Does not consider the management of cost.
- Limited network and does not consider the importance of growing one.
- Does not look for opportunities to increase revenue/make savings.

Technical / Operational Effectiveness

- Describe the steps you regularly take to improve your job performance?
- How do you prioritise your work? Give me an example of where you have had to deal with conflicting priorities/deadlines.
- Describe the project or situation that best demonstrates how you use your analytical abilities.
- Tell me about a project you initiated. How did you organise and schedule the steps involved. What was the outcome?
- Can you give an example of when a project did not go to plan? How did you deal with this?
- What is the most stressful situation you have dealt with in your career? How did you manage it?

Employer Perception: The Negative Indicators

- Lacks an interest in self-improvement – questionable ambition
- Fails to plan ahead.
- Unable to demonstrate initiative
- Finds it difficult to cope under pressure.
- Has failed to stick to plans/budgets and deliverables.

Influence:

- Describe a situation where you were able to influence others on an important issue. What approach or strategy did you use?
- Have you ever had to push an idea through where there was disagreement on approach from other team-members? How did you achieve this?

- Describe a project or idea that you developed that has proven to have had a positive impact within the workplace?
- Describe a time where you failed to get an idea that you knew was the right one. How would you approach this again?
- How much input do you have in your current role?
- Describe when you have used diplomacy to an effective end?

Employer Perception: The Negative Indicators:

- Lacks creativity – avoids sharing ideas
- Shows a lack of ability to influence others
- Does not demonstrate the ability to effect lasting change
- Lacks the initiative to take on responsibilities
- Cannot provide evidence of owning ideas
- Reluctant to voice ideas or share opinions on improving the business.

Motivation

- Where do you see yourself in 5 years' time? What are your career goals?
- What do think the role we are discussing involves?
- What appeals to you about the firm?
- How does this role fit into your overall career plan and why?
- What career options are you considering?
- What aspects of your work do you find most/least satisfying?
- Describe the type of working environment you feel that you would thrive in?
- If you get offers from more than one firm, what criteria will you use to make your decision?

Employer Perception: Negative Indicators

- Limited preparation in advance of the interview.
- Lacks enthusiasm for the role or business unit.
- Has little awareness of what we do
- Lacks focus on career goals and benefit of joining our business
- Lacks drive or enthusiasm for their work
- General sense of lacking ambition

Interviewing If You Were Fired From Your Last Job

If you were fired or 'let go' from your last job then finding a new job will require convincing your future employer that you are not a risky hire. How can you give them confidence that just because things did not work out well in your last job, there should be no reason why this will be a problem now?

The best advice I can give you is to explain the situation honestly. Do not lie. People who concoct stories almost always get found out.

There are 3 main reasons that people get fired:

- Personality clash
- Job Performance
- Gross Misconduct

Personality Clash: This is the easiest of the three to overcome because everyone experiences working with someone they just don't like at some point in their career. When explaining this, it is essential that you remember to be diplomatic. If you didn't like your boss and he/she fired you, explain that over a period of time the relationship diminished and it was just a matter of time before either you left or they let you go. On reflection, you don't wish them ill-will but you would never work for someone like that again.

Job Performance:

If you were fired for poor job performance then I hope the company you worked for had taken you through an appropriate disciplinary process to ensure they gave you every opportunity to improve. If after a period of time you still hadn't met their expectation, then what went wrong? Is this really the best career path for you?

I make this point because if you're applying to work for a similar job, on the same career path, will you perform any better elsewhere? That takes some careful thought prior to an interview because the employer will be thinking about this from the outset and it will be a concern of theirs.

Gross Misconduct:

If you were fired for gross misconduct, then I can only assume you did something very stupid and it cost you your job. Sorry, but it's true and that is also what the employer will think.

Depending on the severity of the incident, the only thing you can do is try and put a positive spin on the whole thing and admit that it is something that you will never do again. Telling a lie at an interview could come back to haunt you – think about this very, very carefully.

Nerves

Ultimately, you have got to quell your nerves and come across credibly. I have seen people become incredibly stressed when having to explain their recent abrupt departure from a company.

I will never forget one guy who spent the entire time I interviewed him, rubbing his thighs and rocking in his seat because he was so nervous about explaining how he got fired from a major bank. He had a personality clash with his line manager and the bank took the decision to get rid of him; really knocking his confidence. Stuff like this happens all the time but it had clearly never happened to him and he was terrified what people might think. I liked him though and I was recruiting for a company that would have been happy to take him on, based on his qualifications and experience. On paper, despite being fired, he was a very strong candidate.

I got him the interview; the feedback was actually quite good but when he had to explain why he'd left his last job, his nerves got the better of him and he panicked. He apparently looked extremely uneasy describing what happened and the rocking, leg-rubbing and facial contortions he displayed really put off his interviewer.

We'd spent a lot of time beforehand, talking about what to say at the interview and he admitted that everything we'd planned just vanished to the point he couldn't explain himself. It got worse by the minute. In the end, he knew he'd blown the interview.

Nerves can be overcome with practice. Enlist the help of a friend or family member to run through a series of mock interviews with you (use the sample questions provided in the Appendix). It would also be good to record the session so you can hear how you responded.

Interviewing If You Were Made Redundant

The big question that goes through the mind of an employer is 'Why were *you* the person they selected for redundancy?'

Every situation is different and the circumstances will always be unique. But over the last 15 years, we've suffered the effects of recessions frequently so it will hardly be a surprise or a concern to an employer that you were one of the people made redundant. Again, positivity needs to be expressed here. You were selected for redundancy amongst others and though it was upsetting, it now gives you the opportunity to take on new challenges and take your career in a different direction.

References

There is a lot of confusion out there about what you should do with references and also what information will be passed from your former employers to your new employer.

On your CV

The general rule of thumb is to never put references on your CV. You have no idea who is going to read your CV at the firm you applied to and you do not want to subject your referees with unnecessary calls. This is even more important if you post your CV on a jobs website - then anyone can ring your referees.

Further, you do not need to put a statement on your CV saying that 'references will be provided on request'. All this does is to make you seem like you have something to hide or that you do not trust people who read your CV. Better to just not mention referees at all.

References from Former Employers

A surprise to many people is that it is illegal in most countries for a firm to give out a bad reference. Data protection and employment laws are there to protect you. Your former employer can only confirm that you worked for the company for the correct time period; that the title of the job you performed is correct and they can confirm the salary details you have provided to the prospective employer is correct. (They do not give out what you were paid; they can only confirm that what you have said is true). Finally, the question will be asked as to whether you would be re-employed in the same role by your old company and they can only state Yes or No. If the answer is No, then it can only mean that you were not a 'good leaver' and there was most likely a problem when you left.

Beware though, well networked line managers can find out information about you very quickly. In many industries, the network of senior managers in competing businesses is very strong. Many worked together at one stage in their career so you could be checked out informally. This is extremely common eg: a mutual former colleague is now working for a completely different firm. Your potential employer calls him or her to discuss what it's like to work with you. Whatever this person says could have a significant impact on whether you get the job or not.

Last Word

I hope you have found the information within this book to be useful. If anything, I hope it has given you an understanding of what to expect at an interview and has forced you to **think** ahead of your next interview.

I run through this process with every candidate I meet and have done for years. The feedback I received throughout has always been that the person had never considered what the employer wanted, nor had they considered the structure that interviews typically follow.

I wish I could tell you that every interview will always follow this structure. A very high percentage will but inevitably, some will veer off the norm. Some employers like to throw curve balls and have some very surprising interview styles, but as I see hundreds of clients and candidates a year, almost all of them agree that interviews do, in the main, follow a similar sequence. Even if the interview veers into something unconventional, the tips in this book have been assembled from a huge range of resources that, though generalist in principle, are also very useful in tackling even an unconventional interview.

Hopefully the importance of preparing for interviews is now fully embedded in your mind and you've picked up and thought about how interviewers will typically engage with you. The simple principle behind interviews is to assess an individual for their ability to undertake a particular job function. But as I've explained, it is the criteria that they use in their selection process that you can use to give you an edge against the competition.

Best of luck in your next interview and remember:

- **Well prepared candidates have more confidence, creating a better first impression.**

- **Well prepared candidates provide better responses to interview questions.**

- **Well prepared candidates get better salary offers**.

Final Recap:

To put it all together and in one place, here are the steps again that summarise the sequence that the interview process follows:

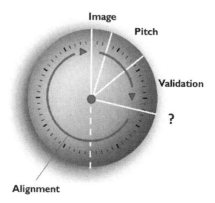

1. What do you know about the company?
2. What do you know about the job?
3. Why are you here?

Strengths:

6 Key Competencies:

1. People Skills
2. Client Focus
3. Commercial Awareness
4. Technical / Operational Effectiveness
5. Influence
6. Motivation

Weakness: Experience – there is always something new to learn

Align your career interests with the job opportunity

Philip Charsley

Acknowledgements

I'd like to thank Ian Clark, Director of Financial Markets at Hays Plc in London for his advice and willingness to cast an eye over my manuscript, despite having an incredibly busy job. You no longer owe me the tie you stole!

More importantly, I'd like to thank my wife Kirstie, for letting me work on this book when I should have been spending time with her and our son Finn - my two favourite people.

Printed in Great Britain
by Amazon